Contents

NEWCASTLE-UNDER-LYME
COLLEGE LEARNING
RESOURCES
fiction Green.

GHOST DOG

Brandon Robshaw

Published in association with
The Basic Skills Agency

Hodder & Stoughton

A MEMBER OF THE HODDER HEADLINE GROUP

Acknowledgements
Cover: James Bartholomew/Photonica
Illustrations: Dave Smith

Orders: please contact Bookpoint Ltd, 130 Milton Park, Abingdon, Oxon OX14 4SB. Telephone: (44) 01235 827720, Fax: (44) 01235 400454. Lines are open from 9.00–6.00, Monday to Saturday, with a 24 hour message answering service.

British Library Cataloguing in Publication Data
A catalogue record for this title is available from The British Library

ISBN 0 340 86949 6

First published 2001
This edition published 2002
Impression number   10 9 8 7 6 5 4 3 2 1
Year   2007 2006 2005 2004 2003 2002

Typeset by SX Composing DTP, Rayleigh, Essex.
Printed in Great Britain for Hodder & Stoughton Educational, a division of Hodder Headline Plc, 338 Euston Road, London NW1 3BH by Athenaeum Press, Gateshead, Tyne & Wear.

1
Noises in the Night

In the middle of the night,
Stan woke up.
He heard a noise.
It was a dog
scratching at his bedroom door.
Whining to be let in.

A chill of fear ran through him.
He pulled the covers over his head.
He lay in bed, stiff and still.
Stan prayed that the whining
and scratching would stop.

It didn't stop.
It went on and on.

Rex wanted to be let in.
Stan knew it was Rex.
He'd know the sound of that dog anywhere.
The sound of it broke his heart.

He ought to get up
and let Rex in.
Let Rex curl up on his bed,
like the old times.

But still he lay there
in the dark, without moving.

He couldn't let Rex in.
He didn't dare.
He didn't want to see what Rex looked like.
Because Rex had been dead for a year.
He knew that for a fact.

2
Rex and Stan

Rex and Stan went back a long way.
Rex was a puppy when Stan got him.
He was a black mongrel
with a rough coat.
He had long legs
and a white mark on his chest.

Stan lived on his own.
A dog was just what he needed
for company.
He loved Rex.
'You're my best friend,'
he used to say to him.
Stan was rather a lonely man.

He took Rex out for long walks
whenever he could.
The only trouble was,
he was out at work all day.
He worked for a company that made
dog food, funnily enough.
He was out from eight in the morning
until six in the evening.
It was a long time to leave Rex alone.
But what could he do?

Rex didn't like being left alone.
He barked a lot.

Sometimes he tore up
the chairs and cushions.
Stan used to get angry about this
and smack him.
But it wasn't really Rex's fault,
Stan knew that.
Rex got bored and lonely during the day.
Stan wasn't happy to leave him,
but he had no choice.
He had to work.

At least Rex knew he would always come
back.
Rex would jump for joy when he came home.
Stan would feed him
and take him for a long walk.
At night, Rex slept on his bed.

It went on like that for six years.
Until one day Stan had to go to Manchester
for a training day.

3
Jill

_____

It was his company's idea.
He didn't want to go.
He had to catch a train there.
He knew he wouldn't be home till late.
It was a long time to leave Rex alone.

Stan's company said he had to go.
So he left plenty of food and water for Rex.

He said 'Goodbye.'
Rex looked at him with sad brown eyes.
'Don't worry,' said Stan.
'I'll be back tonight. Promise.'
As he closed the door,
Rex started to whine.

The training day was a waste of time.
Well, Stan knew it would be.
It was all about working in teams
to get new ideas.

The leader put them into groups.
He said their plane had crashed
on a mountain.
They had to work out a way of getting down.
What a waste of time, thought Stan.
He just wanted to be at home with his dog.

'Isn't this silly?' said a woman in his group.
Stan liked the look of her.
She was very pretty.
She had blonde hair and green eyes.
She looked a bit like a cat.

'Yes, it's a waste of time,' said Stan.
They both laughed.
'I'm Jill,' said the woman.
'I'm Stan,' said Stan.

They sat together at lunch.
'What does your company sell?'
Stan asked her.
'Bras,' said Jill.
For some reason,
Stan felt his face going red.

'What about your company?' asked Jill.
'Dog food,' said Stan.
Jill laughed.
'What's funny?' asked Stan.
'I don't know,' said Jill.

They were in different groups
in the afternoon.
Stan's group had to work out how to cross
a river with crocodiles in it.

At the end of the day Jill came up to him.
'Fancy a drink?' she asked.

4
A Quick Drink

'I'd love to,' said Stan.
'But I can't. I've got a train to catch.'

'So catch the next one.'

'I've got to get home to my dog.'

'Well, he'll still be there when you get back,
won't he?' said Jill.
'Come on. Just a quick drink.'

Stan looked at her.
She really was very pretty.
'Well . . . OK,' he said. 'Just one.'

If he caught the next train,
he'd be home by nine o'clock.
That wasn't too bad.

They had a great time in the pub.
They got on like a house on fire.
They made each other laugh.
They had one drink. Then another.
Then one more.
'Where are you from?' Stan asked.
'You sound Scottish.'

'I am. I'm from Dundee,' said Jill.
'I came down on the train.
I'm staying in a hotel tonight.
Where are you from?'

'London. I live there with my dog.'

Jill laughed.
'You love your dog, don't you?'
'I bet you'd rather be with him than me.'

'I didn't say that.'

'Have another drink, then.'

Stan looked at his watch.
Then he jumped to his feet.
'It's nine o'clock!
I'm late!
I'll have to go right now –
or I'll miss the last train!'

'Oh, all right,' said Jill.
She looked disappointed.
'I won't keep you from your dog.
Look, here's my number.
Call me some time.
We could meet again.
Maybe I could meet your dog!'

Jill smiled,
waiting for Stan to kiss her goodbye.
But Stan just turned and ran out of the pub.
He mustn't miss that last train!

5
Crash!

Stan ran to the station as fast as he could.
He was only just in time.
The London train was just about to leave.
Stan ran and threw himself onto the train.
Made it!

The train moved off.
Stan sat back in his seat.
He watched the countryside go by.
He felt a bit better now.
He'd left Rex alone a long time,
but he'd be home by midnight.

Then he would make it up to Rex.
He would take him for a long walk.
Cook him some chicken.
Give him some chocolate.
Rex would be so pleased to see him . . .

Stan started to think about Jill.
She had seemed to like him.
Maybe he should call her.
Dundee was a long way,
but he could go and stay for a weekend.
Rex would love it up there.
All that open space.

Stan started to feel pretty happy.
It would be good to have a woman in his life . . .

There was a loud bang and a sudden jolt.
Stan was thrown out of his seat.
He hit his head. He felt a sharp pain.
Then everything went black.

6

In Hospital

Stan opened his eyes. He was in bed.
His head was hurting.
A woman in a white coat
was sitting by the side of the bed.

'Where am I?' asked Stan.

'In hospital,' said the woman. 'Don't worry.
You're going to be all right.
I'm Dr Foster, by the way.'

'I'm Stan,' said Stan.
'What happened?'

'There was a train crash,' said Dr Foster.
'You hit your head quite badly.
You're lucky to be alive.'

'Yes,' said Stan.
Suppose he had died?
Then Rex would have starved to death.
A chill ran through him just thinking of it.
'Listen, Doctor, I've got to get home.
As soon as possible.'

'I wouldn't advise moving just yet,'
said Dr Foster. 'You need to rest.'

'You don't understand. I've got to get back.
My dog is waiting for me.'

'All the same,
I wouldn't advise leaving just yet.
You've just come out of a coma.'

'A coma?' said Stan.

'That's right. So you do need to rest.'

Fear came into Stan's eyes.
He gripped the Doctor's arm.
'How long?
How long was I in a coma?'

'Two weeks,' said Dr Foster.

7

A New House

Stan never went home after that.
He just couldn't face it.
He didn't want to see
what had happened to Rex.

Rex must be dead, of course.
Stan had left him some food and water,
but only enough for a day.
Not enough for two weeks.

Rex had to be dead.
A dog might – just might –
live for two weeks without food.
But not without water.
No animal could live for two weeks
without water.

Stan just couldn't bear
to see his thin, stiff little body.
So he never went home.
He didn't own the house.
He was only renting it.
He just found another house
and started renting that.

He left all his stuff behind.
He had to buy new clothes,
new shoes, a new CD player,
a new TV.
But he didn't care.
He felt too bad
to care about anything much.

He told himself it wasn't his fault.
He didn't know the train
was going to crash, did he?
But if he hadn't gone for a drink with Jill,
he wouldn't have been on that train.
He would have been on the earlier one.
That bit was his fault.
Stan couldn't forget what he had done.
He couldn't stop blaming himself.

8

Rex Comes Back

A year later, Stan lay in bed.
He knew what the date was.
Exactly a year ago today,
he had gone to Manchester
and left Rex to die.
He couldn't stop thinking about it.

He closed his eyes and tried to sleep.
That was when the whining started.
And the scratching at the door.

It was Rex, he knew it was Rex.
Yet it couldn't be Rex.
Rex was dead.

The whining and the scratching went on and
on.
'Please!' Stan called out.
'Leave me alone!
Leave me in peace!'

At the sound of his master's voice,
Rex whined and scratched even louder.

It was a long night for Stan.
He didn't sleep a wink.

Morning came.

Now the whining and scratching
would stop, Stan hoped.
Ghosts weren't supposed to hang around
in the daytime.

The whining and scratching didn't stop.
It went on and on.
All day.
Stan couldn't bear it.
Yet he couldn't get up and open the door.
He didn't dare.
The ghost of Rex would be hungry.
He might tear Stan's throat out.

'Go away!' called Stan. 'Please, Rex!'
Rex didn't go away.
He kept whining and scratching.

Stan was trapped.
He couldn't leave the room.
He was trapped there with no food or water.

It was a long day.
Then night fell.
Then another day
and another night.
And still Rex waited outside the door.

9

Dead in Bed

They found Stan dead in bed
two weeks later.
The police broke the door down.
The neighbours had complained
about the smell.

Stan's body was as thin as a skeleton.
He had had no food or water
for two weeks.
A man might live for two weeks without
food.
But not without water.

No one could understand
why he had died.
He wasn't locked in.
He could have gone to get
food and water.
Instead, he had stayed in bed
and starved to death.

There was one other strange thing.
The police heard a dog barking
when they broke down the door.
But when they got in,
they couldn't find a dog anywhere.